Perfect

Nikki Basta

BookLeaf
Publishing

India | USA | UK

Presentation by *BookLeaf Publishing*

Web: www.bookleafpub.com

E-mail: info@bookleafpub.com

ISBN: 9789363310353

First edition 2024

This book is for You.

ACKNOWLEDGEMENT

Thank you to all who I come from,
Thank you to all who I've met.
You've molded my being,
I owe a great debt.

PREFACE

I knew that I would never share anything with the world unless it was perfect.
So I named this book of poems, "Perfect", and now it is here.
Consider it divinely inspired.

I Met God On A Thursday

One summer evening
just before the 18th hour
In the Valley of Wind
bloomed the tiniest flower

And from the dust
from which she settled
Gaia breathed a song
into her petals

God was there
sitting under the oak tree
God was there
and he welcomed me

Summer flower
was late to bloom
It was by design
threads in the loom

And when the summer
Became the Fall
There came a time
To experience it all

For across the way
Just past the oak tree
Seven valleys
outstretched before me

God was there
as I peaked over the wall
Oh, how He knew
I would answer the call

I slowly descended
into the Valley of One
And followed a path
that faced the Sun

With no compass on my person
And no map in my hand
I walked by faith
for God knew the land

And in the deepest cave
At the furthest point
Just when I had tired
In my quest to anoint

I opened my eye
In the dark I could see
That I must give
What I most need

I met God again on a Tuesday
Sitting once more under the oak tree
Gaia raised another flower
This time, to be greeted by me.

A Time Of Compassion

Through twists of fate
Of love and hate
I will restate
My own innate

I know I'm late
I'm sorry mate
Forgot the date
And time I ate

I'm at the gate
Please don't debate
My heart's true weight
My faith is straight

Because this time…
This, time…
it's not about perfection…

It's about compassion.

The Scenic Route

5

Life has gotten way too heavy
I fear I'll give way to the levy

So time it is to change my pace
And put a smile upon my face

For I'm too tired to race and race
I am a tortoise, I move with grace

I no longer care what you might say
I wander Earth, I like it this way

For now my heart is light and airy
Singing songs, a yellow canary
Have a seat and let's be merry
And watch the sunset on the prairie.

The Mountain Cries Out

The ancient mountain
In the valley of One
Thousands of years
under the Golden Sun

But it is the Silvery Moon
who saw it all
In the darkest night
spring tears did fall

For the Mountain was wise
And tough as can be
No one could move it
Except the powers to be

But the mountain could feel
From the tiniest feet
A need to heal
And a need to retreat

For the Mountain loves people
And welcomed them all
To see what it sees
And to answer the call

But not all were lighthearted
Not all were aligned
Some were retarded
And some were not kind

For the mountain springs
Began to run dry
What was once abundant
Till the gold miners arrived

And for this reason
The Mountain did cry
For he feared this season
His heart would die

Can We go Home Now?

My hand gripped tightly around a stone
To fling is all I've ever known
Up at the donkey and elephant, too
Welcome to the circus, this ain't no zoo.

For this is all a wack display
Of red against blue
Of black against white
You win or you lose

A tired old system
Of war and of hate
Are we done with this program?
It's starting to get late

Oh, how we are sick!
Of mind and of body
Our media is quick
To make scandal a hobby

We fight and we plead
"Turn off the machine!"
Oh, how desperation
Breeds a society, diseased

Our system is old

Our system is doomed
It knows only survival
It does not know bloom

Is this all we have?
Our people are halved!
Are we not more advanced?
Have we danced our last dance?

We have more in us, truly
To make things less unruly
You can keep all your jewelry
This won't be done cruelly

In every glyph you will surely read
A system of love is what we need
To heal the sick we must proceed
To put an end to all this greed

Why did we forget about us?
Why did we decide to ditch trust?
Why entertain all this fuss?
When integrity is a must!

And now I ask, who will it be?
Who will be first, you or me?
To look at their stone and say, "Gee..
Perhaps I'll build a home with this…
And set myself free."

Old Plate

I stumbled down the mountain
And I dropped my goddamn plate
Away went all my cherries
That's what I get for being late!

My plate rolled to the river
Clear waters cleaned its slate
That's when I saw the glimmer
Of gold patterns, so ornate!

Upon green banks it landed
In such a perfect state
I kissed the plate all over
And shouted, "God is Great!"

A voice then answered back to me
"You know, you're never late.
You're just on time my darling,
Now go, fill up that plate."

Now I turned to face the big wide world
And with my golden plate
I shouted out so happily,
"I can't wait to have a taste!"

The Answer

Who, if I cried out,
Would save me from the cliff I dangle?

Who, if I cried out,
Would pull away the hands that strangle?

Who, if I cried out,
Would cut away my ropes all tangled?

Who, if I cried out,
Would patch my body up all mangled?

Who, if I cried out,
would answer me among the angels?

But, no, please no
Don't take my devils away
For in this song
They have their role to play

One day, One day
The sun will come up
And I will fly away
With my golden cup

For my devils and angels
Have taught me the way
All paths lead to God
And with gratitude, I pay.

Blessed

Well, I found God there
And I found God here
And from here to there
I found God everywhere!

For I don't fear the serpent
With my faith I'm devote
That even in the snake pit
I will find the antidote!

For God is everywhere
the eye can see
He's here for you
and he's here for me!

For any man who searches,
Blessed is he!

Two Snakes

Two snakes within me
One black, One white
They dance together
In the dark and the light

At first I was scared
For the serpent might bite
At first I was scared
Because of Adam's sight

But as I peered
Into the Black Serpent's eye
I saw chaos all around
And the soul's dark night

And when I gazed
Into the White Serpent's eye
I saw order and reason
In all of God's might

The tradition in me
Demanded I resist temptation
But the Spirit in me
Encouraged communication

And from the forked tongues
Of Two serpents
I heard a timeless story
And began my repentance

The Melody I heard
Made my body quake
For my walls began to crumble
My spirit was AWAKE

I saw the truth
I saw the slight
I saw the HARMONY
Of dark and light

From the serpents' tongue
I entered the abyss
Where a golden apple
Lay amiss

I picked up the apple
And split it in two
And I found a black seed
Now, what to do?

I returned to Eden
And I found good dirt
I grabbed a shovel
And I hiked up my skirt

I planted the seed
And watched curiously
As an Apple tree sprout up
With tremendous velocity

And from this tree
I gathered more seed
And planted more trees
As far as the eye can see

And when the day was done
And my long hair hung
I looked to find the hungry…
Not a single one.

And now I know
And now I see
The apple is for You
The apple is for Me

For the serpents have taught
This ignorant girl
That God will not leave you
Not in His world

And in His world he shed the light
And in His world he created the night
For the Seeker becomes the Master
Once fear takes flight.

Forget About It

Forget the house!
Forget the car!
Are you at PEACE
With who you are?

Empty Fields Full of Stories

Oh, how I love a good story!
From every downfall
To every glory!
From my lovely neighbor
Or from the stars' quarry
I will hear it through
Don't you worry

For I am the Story Collector
I listen now
With all your specters
I hear the tale
In all your lectures
I see the movement
Through all the pictures

I look in your eyes
And I see every line
I hold your hands
And I hear every rhyme
I listen to your heart
Even if you're not mine
I will carry your voice
Even if you're a mime

For I am the Story Keeper
I don't float on the surface
I always swim deeper
Even when you don't notice

Because our stories are bigger
Than just you and just me
Our stories bang and they knock
And they shout, "I have the key!"

For I am the StoryTeller
And I walk through each field
From the dust I remember
All the fruit that you yield

With obsidian in my left hand
And Opal in the other
I carry the stories
Of every sister and every brother.

Legacy

Glory and legacy
became my obsession
I wanted to last
To leave an impression

As I built my temple
From stone and from quartz
I noticed a wobble
And down came my supports

I lashed and I anguished
As I continued to fall
Life has been wasted
To hell with it all!

For death was all I feared
I did not want to disappear
Am I worthy to hear?
Am I even worth a tear?

Then BOOM! Came the thunder
And ZOW! Came the lightning
For God saw my heart
It was time for enlightening

He hurled me into the heavens
Where I sat and I watched
As God poured our souls
Right into Earth's crotch

I watched as the souls
Spread all around the globe
Transformed over time
The earth was aglow

For Gaia loves us so
And as she looked up with glee
I was humbled in her eyes
For in them, I saw me

And God gently spoke,
"Now, do you see?"
You are not playing the long game
You are playing for eternity
And you are never alone
For you have me
Now return back to Earth
And show me you're free

My toes kissed the dust
And my curls touched the wind
My eyes looked beyond
For the veil was now thinned

I saw in every flower,
every rock and tree
A reflection of you
and a reflection of me
And a sound promise
of everlasting glory
For In every dew drop
there, was our story

Now I sing to my people
With keen apparentness
God and His green Earth
Are my only inheritance.

I Am

When the day's begun
I will greet the sun
With my little one
It will be done

She will greet the trees
And greet the bees
And feel the breeze
And sit with ease

I will let her know
As long as flowers grow
And peaks have snow
And the rivers flow
And the sun does glow
She will never be alone

For I am in the stars
And I am in your scars
And I am in your hair
And I am everywhere

Don't miss me long
For I am not gone
And I will return
For this world, I yearn.

Equals

In all my years
The largest of crows
Were simply in my own backyard

I would chase them screaming
Fists clenched
Hoping to ward them off for good

Time and time again
They would return to my yard
Never making a sound

I cried to God,
"Please! Take them away!"
One day, one day

Oh, but Today…
I opened my eyes
To the sun up above and all of its love

I watched the rays of light
Dance across their shiny backs
Blacks and blues and indigo

With a sigh, I entered my yard once more
Eyes level
Fists clenched

Only, this time they would be opened…
Arms extended…
Fingers spilling over with birdseed

I am wiser, now, and I have to say,
"Thank you, dear crow…
And welcome home."

Kindness, First

A little child
So free and wild
Was asked about her future

What will you be
When you're thirty three
And please don't say, "A Moocher"

She sat and pondered
While they wondered
If she'll sew up sutures

She said, "I'll be kind!"
They said, "She's lost her mind!"
And quickly called a tutor.

It's All Good, Really

To all my heartbreakers,
I harbor no hate or ill wishes.
I felt I'd given my best to pull you over the cliff
from which you dangle,
And in the end…
As the current pulled me under…
Darker, deeper, darker, deeper I fell,
As my heart desperately gagged my screams
Of horror as I realized the betrayal
That was now my reality…
I saw it.
I saw the glimmer of horror, shame, regret,
shock…
Even fear…
I saw the scared child in your eyes.
Those eyes whispered a quiet fear, a cry for help,
a woeful apology.
In them I saw Lucifer, light succumbed to
darkness like a man to the succubus.
And while darkness does exist,
And we see it in every brother and sister,
Mother and father, friend or foe…
That is not the focal point of the story.
For these words glow by the candlelight of
Compassion and forgiveness.

Of the elevated station.
A "what would Jesus do" bracelet made of dark
brown leather wound sung around my throat -
and not tightly, no.
Rather, I am bound in faith and HONOR.
It rests like a butterfly in my shoulders,
As light as a feather adorned with beautifully
reflective iridescent sheer and fluffy white tuft.

I forgive you child.
For a man to commit such darkness upon
another… that is a boy who has known nothing
else. And my heart weeps for you… and all the
children of this world who were raised up in
darkness... who have forgotten their light.

My Dragon

Before our paths crossed,
death was not an unwelcome friend to me.
You see, I had made peace by the age of seven
and the great dark mystery of the cosmos
beckoned me.

I was grateful for all that this green earth had
abundantly showered me with,
experiences of the brightest highs and the lowest
lows.
I did not mind if the Great Spirit called me home
early
Even without notice, not one bit.

But then I stared into the moss-covered
red rocks embedded in earth's dark, rich soil
with the clearest spring streams running over
them.
Spring streams that came from the winter cold
melting away in the warmth of the sun.
Beautiful and inviting,
with a slight chill to the touch and deceptively
deeper
than one's first impression.

Yes, losing myself in your eyes came as
naturally
as the winter loses itself to spring.
I was a phenomenon that could not be resisted.
A cycle that I felt was not bound by a single
lifetime, no.
I had - we had - certainly been in this season
many times before,
and would be infinitely into the future.

Then suddenly, I experience a feeling that held
little to no space
in my flesh before...
I didn't want to die.
How could I?
I'd only just found this familiar spirit,
a connection so rare and unfathomable
that I could hardly believe the possibility of this
miracle ever existed.

I had discovered a thing of legends...
He was my very own dragon.

Victory of the People

I am not a victim in this life,
I am the victor!

Despite it all
I answered the call

I have gratitude for my past
And hope for my future

I am Victory of the People,
And it is so nice to meet you.

www.ingramcontent.com/pod-product-compliance
Lightning Source LLC
LaVergne TN
LVHW010939200726
843509LV00013B/2253